Don't buy two copies of this book. Take the child on your lap as you read to him, and let him have the fun of reading to you. If he is in the first grade he can read to you, for every other poem is written in a basic first-grade vocabulary, and you can help with a slightly harder word here and there.

There are two kinds of children's books. There are read-to-me books, and there are I-can-read-to-you books. This one is a combination. If you will read the first poem to him, he (or, of course, she) will be able to read the next poem to you. And so on.

You read to me,

I'll read to you

BY JOHN CIARDI

DRAWINGS BY EDWARD GOREY

HarperTrophy
A Division of HarperCollins*Publishers*

Contents

All the poems printed in black, you read to me.

Contents

All the poems printed in blue, I'll read to you.

ABOUT THE TEETH OF SHARKS

The thing about a shark is—teeth,
One row above, one row beneath.

Now take a close look. Do you find
It has another row behind?

Still closer—here, I'll hold your hat:
Has it a third row behind that?

Now look in and . . . Look out! Oh my,
I'll *never* know now! Well, goodbye.

I WOULDN'T

There's a mouse house
In the hall wall
With a small door
By the hall floor
Where the fat cat
Sits all day,
Sits that way
All day
Every day
Just to say,
"Come out and play"
To the nice mice
In the mouse house
In the hall wall
With the small door
By the hall floor.

And do they
Come out and play
When the fat cat
Asks them to?

Well, would you?

ARVIN MARVIN LILLISBEE FITCH

Arvin Marvin Lillisbee Fitch
Rode a broomstick like a witch.
Out the window, over the trees,
Above the hills, across two seas,
And up and up on a wild moonbeam
Till he came to the other side of his dream,
Where he bumped his head a terrible thump
On the top of the dark, and fell *ker-flump!*—
Down, down, down, down like a piece of lead,
Till he landed—*thud!*—in his very own bed.

He didn't cry. He didn't scream,
He simply said, "When next I dream,
It seems to me it might be wise
To keep my dreams a smaller size."

So saying, he went back to sleep
And dreamed about such things as sheep,
And birthday parties, and buttercups,
And toothpaste tubes, and spotted pups—
Good proper dreams, and none so tall
That he ran any risk of a fall.

Arvin's dreams were beautiful,
But perhaps a little dull.
In fact, but for the birthday cake
He might as well have stayed awake.
And in his sleep I heard him sigh,
"It was more fun when I dreamed high!"

WOULDN'T YOU?

If I
Could go
As high
And low
As the wind
As the wind
As the wind
Can blow—

I'd go!

MIND YOU, NOW

Never stroll away from camp
Without a brush, a comb,
A compass, and a postage stamp
To mail yourself back home.

Don't go off to Oregon
Without at least one shoe,
Or you may get a blister on
Your toe—or even two.

Don't go past the Golden Gate
Without a dinner pail,
A pillow, and your hat on straight,
And a ship in which to sail.

Or long before you reach the land
You may find that you will get
Hungry, sleepy, sunburned, and
Both your feet extremely wet.

WHAT NIGHT WOULD IT BE?

If the moon shines
On the black pines
And an owl flies
And a ghost cries
And the hairs rise
On the back
    on the back
        on the back of your neck—

If you look quick
At the moon-slick
On the black air
And what goes there
Rides a broom-stick
And if things pick
At the back
    at the back
        at the back of your neck—

Would you know then
By the small men
With the lit grins
And with no chins,
By the owl's *hoo,*
And the ghost's *boo,*

By the Tom Cat,
And the Black Bat
On the night air,
And the thing there,
By the thing,
     by the thing,
          by the dark thing there

(Yes, you do,
     yes, you do
          know the thing I mean)

That it's now,
     that it's now,
          that it's—Halloween!

MUMMY SLEPT LATE AND
DADDY FIXED BREAKFAST

Daddy fixed the breakfast.
He made us each a waffle.
It looked like gravel pudding.
It tasted something awful.

"Ha, ha," he said, "I'll try again.
This time I'll get it right."
But what *I* got was in between
Bituminous and anthracite.

"A little too well done? Oh well,
I'll have to start all over."
That time what landed on my plate
Looked like a manhole cover.

I tried to cut it with a fork:
The fork gave off a spark.
I tried a knife and twisted it
Into a question mark.

I tried it with a hack-saw.
I tried it with a torch.
It didn't even make a dent.
It didn't even scorch.

The next time Dad gets breakfast
When Mommy's sleeping late,
I think I'll skip the waffles.
I'd sooner eat the plate!

LITTLE BITS

"Will you have some pie?"
Said Jane. Said I,
"Well, just a little. Just a bit."
But I found when I had eaten it
That just *one* little-bit wouldn't do.
So I told Jane to make it *two*.

Then was I happy with what I got?
Well, little-bits can't make a lot.
For little-bits are small, you see.
So I told Jane to make it *three*.

Three little-bits are not much more
Than *two*. So I said, "Make it *four*."

And I ate them up. Then asked for *five*.
Then *six*. Till Jane said, "Sakes alive,
Here are two more and that makes *eight*.
If you don't stop you'll eat the plate!"
"*Eight* little-bits," I said, "are fine.
But would you care to make it *nine*?"

Said Jane, "I'd make it *forty-four*.
But, sad to say, there are no more.
By little-bit and little-bit
You've eaten all there was of it.

I know that little-bits are small.
But a lot of little-bits is *all*.
And little by little by little, you see,
Gets down to none at all for me!

That's why I hope that when I bake
Another pie, you will just take
One great big fat thick lot of it,
And let me have a little-bit!"

ABOUT JIMMY JAMES

Jimmy James when he was three
Tried to run away to sea,
Got his feet wet in the foam,
Had to turn and go back home.

He tried to run away once more
To join the army when he was four.
Alas, the General made him pack
His bubble-gum and go right back.

At five he tried to catch a train
But gave it up because of rain.
(At six and seven he tried again
But got a cinder in his eye
And had to run back home to cry.)

At eight he kicked up such a fuss
His parents put him on a bus
With eighteen cents, a ball of twine,
And transfers to another line.
They went home feeling rather fine.

But Jimmy came back home at nine.
His father groaned, his mother sighed.
His sister just sat down and cried.
Still Jimmy wasn't satisfied.

At ten, to everyone's delight,
He stole out of the house one night
And, this time, ran away for good,
Taking the short cut through the wood.

That's what he did. But sad to say
He met a tiger on the way.
Though in justice I must add
The tiger acted rather glad.

What Jimmy felt is not quite clear:
It was a little hard to hear
Just what he had to say, because
When talking past a tiger's jaws
One's best remarks may be cut off
By a yawn or sneeze or cough.

And the whole conversation stops
When the tiger licks his chops.

THE WISE HEN

A fox and a hen went out one day.
They met somewhere along the way.
Said the fox, "I am happy we two met.
Just look at that cloud. You are going to get wet
If you stay out here—that's plain to see.
I beg you to come along home with me."

The hen looked up at that cloud in the sky
And said, "It is true I like to be dry.
But as for going home with you—
You are kind, dear sir, to ask me to,
And I want to say I am glad we met.
But if you don't mind, I will just get wet,
And then get dry as best I can.
So good day to you, sir."

                    And away she ran.

A COOL DRINK ON A HOT DAY

The Hoo-hah and the Rinky-dink
    And the Automatic Chugg
Were sitting around—in a fog, I think—
Mixing chocolate mud and lemon ink
To make themselves a good cool drink
    Inside a cider jug.

They had tons and tons and tons of ice
    And plenty of mud, do you see?
But the ink ran low, and once or twice
The Rinky-dink stopped to ask for advice
From the Automatic Chugg. "Use spice,
    If we're out of ink," said he.

"There's pepper and mustard and garlic, too.
    And plenty of dynamite dust.
And some rocket fuel. If that won't do,
All I can say is, it's up to you.
Or, if you're desperate, ask the Hoo."
    "Ask," said the Hoo, "if you must."

"Well, then, I must," said the Rinky-dink.
    "Hah!" said the Hoo, "you're a fool!
Why should you bother to ask what I think?
I never did care for lemon ink.
The one thing to think about mixing a drink
    Is simply to make it cool."

"If you can't make it cool, don't stand there and bawl,"
    Said the Hoo-hah, nibbling his mug.
"Your tears are too salty. Just look at them fall!
Well, if you insist, I suggest that you call
For some worthless advice from the best of us all,
    Which, such as it is, is the Chugg."

But the Chugg, though he spoke, had nothing to say
    Except, "My, the fog's getting thick.
I really believe that's enough for today.
What I suggest is you throw it away.
Besides, if we drink it, I half think we may
    Discover the stuff makes us sick."

So the Chugg and the Hoo and the Rinky-dink,
    As nearly as I recall,
Had little to eat and nothing to drink.
They would have gone home rather thirsty, I think.
Except that the fog had grown darker than ink
    And they couldn't go home at all.

ONE DAY

I lay in the grass and looked at the sky.
My, how the clouds were running by!
They were big as a house! They were big as a hill!
But they all ran by as still as still
                    TILL
The wind blew into the biggest cloud.
The cloud grew black. The cloud grew loud.
The cloud lit up with a mile-long flash.
Then all the top of the sky went CRASH!
And then with a hiss as loud as a jet
The water came down like strings of wet.
Did I say strings? It was more like rocks!
It filled my shoes! It wet my socks!

I ran for home. The whole cloud shook
With a *crash-bang-bang,* and a big bright hook
Ripped out from the sky. And then a brook
Began to run from the end of my nose
To my chin, to my neck, right down to my toes.
I ran and I ran but I couldn't begin
To run as fast as my nose and chin.
I ran. Oh, I ran! And I forget
When I got home. But I know *how*—wet!

GIRL

ALL ABOUT BOYS AND GIRLS

I know all about boys, I do,
And I know all about little girls, too.
I know what they eat. I know what they drink.
I know what they like. I know what they think.

And so I'm writing this to say,
Don't let children out to play.
It makes them sad. They'd rather go
To school or to the dentist. Oh,

I know they're bashful about saying
How much it hurts to be out playing
When they could go to school and spell
And mind their manners. They won't tell

How tired they are of games and toys.
But I know girls, and I know boys.
They like to sweep floors, chop the wood,
And practice being very good.

They'd rather sit and study hard
Than waste the whole day in the yard.
What good is fun and making noise?
That's not for girls! That's not for boys!

SOMETIMES I FEEL THIS WAY

I have one head that wants to be good,
    And one that wants to be bad.
And always, as soon as I get up,
    One of my heads is sad.

"Be bad," says one head. "Don't you know
    It's fun to be bad. Be as bad as you like.
Put sand in your brother's shoe—that's fun.
    Put gum on the seat of your sister's bike."

"What fun is that?" says my other head.
    "Why not go down before the rest
And set things out for breakfast? My,
    That would please Mother. Be good—that's best."

"What! Better than putting frogs in the sink?
    Or salt in the tea-pot? Have some fun.
Be bad, be bad, be good and bad.
    You know it is good to be bad," says One.

"Is it good to make Sister and Brother sad?
    And Mother and Daddy? And when you do,
Is it good to get spanked? Is it good to cry?
    No, no. Be good—that's best," says Two.

So one by one they say what they say,
    And what they say is "Be Good—Be Bad."
And if One is happy that makes Two cry.
    And if Two is happy that makes One sad.

Someday maybe, when I grow up,
    I shall wake and find I have just one—
The happy head. But which will it be?
    I wish I knew. They are both *some* fun.

31

THE JOURNEY

I went through a forest without a tree
By a river that was dry.
I came to a shore without a sea.
I hurried right on by.

I came to a town that had no street,
No houses, and no stores,
And no one you would care to meet,
Not in nor out of doors.

I spoke to a woman who had no name.
"How do you do?" said I.
"I wish you, sir, the very same,"
Was all she would reply.

"Is there any to speak to here?"
"No one to speak of," said she,
"But why not try Minnie McGinnis, my dear?
—The which, of course, is me."

I asked her a question that had no end.
She answered without a start.
"You had best ask Minnie McGinnis, my friend.
She has a kindly heart."

She gave me directions that made no sense.
I came to where I was not.
I passed through a gate built in no fence
To a house without a lot.

I entered the house that could not be.
A draft that caused no stir.
Rustled a curtain I could not see.
The curtain became a blur.

And there stood no one at all—unless
It was Minnie McGinnis, and she
All done up in her wedding dress
With a groom that, of course, was me.

THE LIGHT-HOUSE-KEEPER'S WHITE-MOUSE

As I rowed out to the light-house
For a cup of tea one day,
I came on a very wet white-mouse
Out swimming in the bay.

"If you are for the light-house,"
Said he, "I'm glad we met.
I'm the light-house-keeper's white-mouse
And I fear I'm getting wet."

"O light-house-keeper's white-mouse,
I am rowing out for tea
With the keeper in his light-house.
Let me pull you in with me."

So I gave an oar to the white-mouse.
And I pulled on the other.
And we all had tea at the light-house
With the keeper and his mother.

CHANG McTANG McQUARTER CAT

Chang McTang McQuarter Cat
Is one part this and one part that.
One part is yowl, one part is purr.
One part is scratch, one part is fur.
One part, maybe even two,
Is how he sits and stares right through
You and you and you and you.
And when you feel my Chang-Cat stare
You wonder if you're really there.

Chang McTang McQuarter Cat
Is one part this and ten parts that.
He's one part saint, and two parts sin.
One part yawn, and three parts grin,
One part sleepy, four parts lightning,
One part cuddly, five parts fright'ning,
One part snarl, and six parts play.
One part is how he goes away
Inside himself, somewhere miles back
Behind his eyes, somewhere as black
And green and yellow as the night
A jungle makes in full moonlight.

Chang McTang McQuarter Cat
Is one part this and twenty that.
One part is statue, one part tricks—
(One part, or six, or thirty-six.)

One part (or twelve, or sixty-three)
Is—Chang McTang belongs to ME!

Don't ask, "How many parts is that?"
Addition's nothing to a cat.

If you knew Chang, then you'd know this:
He's one part everything there is.

MY CAT, MRS. LICK-A-CHIN

Some of the cats I know about
Spend a little time in and a lot of time out.
Or a lot of time out and a little time in.
But *my* cat, Mrs. Lick-a-chin,
Never knows *where* she wants to be.
If I let her in she looks at me
And begins to sing that she wants to go out.
So I open the door and she looks about
And begins to sing, "Please let me in!"

Poor silly Mrs. Lick-a-chin!

The thing about cats, as you may find,
Is that no one knows what they have in mind.

And I'll tell you something about that:
No one knows it less than my cat.

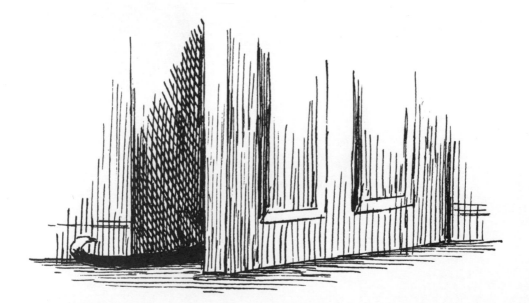

A SAD SONG

I had two eels once that I taught
To make themselves a true love-knot.
But one would slip and one would slide,
And the knot would come untied.
No matter that I tried and tried.
No matter even that I cried.
The knot would always come untied.

Eels, perhaps, are poor at tying
Knots, or knots are not worth trying.
I tried by patient scholarship
To teach my eels the proper grip.
But one would slide and one would slip,
Or one would slip and one would slide,
And the knot would come untied.

No matter that I tried and tried.
No matter even that I cried.
The knot would always come untied.

A SEA SONG

There was a man out your way
Who took a ship to sea.
He set out, I'm told, for Norway,
Packed full of T.N.T.

A fog blew up. He lost his head.
(With his hat on, so they say.)
"Oh dear, I cannot find," he said,
"My hat, nor head, nor way!"

He lost his way, his head, his hat
And hit a rock off Finland.
The T.N.T. blew up at that
With a bang heard ten miles inland.

He lost his way, his head, his hat.
What more is there to say?
Don't go to sea with T.N.T.
Or your hat may blow away.

HOW TO TELL A TIGER

People who know tigers
    Very very well
All agree that tigers
    Are not hard to tell.

The way to tell a tiger is
    With lots of room to spare.
Don't try telling them up close
    Or we may not find you there.

MY HORSE, JACK

My horse, Jack, ran off to sea.
In ten years he came back to me
With a smell of salt and a smell of tar
And three little sea-horses swimming in a jar.

He ate my oats and he ate my hay
And he did no work and all he'd say
Was "I met my love when the sea was blue.
I loved her. She loved me true.

I lost my love when the sea was black.
She swam away and she never swam back.
So I tucked my babies into a jar
And here I am and here they are."

And he ate my oats and he ate my hay
And he did no work, and that's all he'd say.

A WARNING ABOUT BEARS

Some bears are fierce, and most grow fiercer
When any one bites off their ears, sir.
With bears it's best to be polite.
And a bit distant—that's all right.
But, please, when meeting bears, don't bite.

MORE ABOUT BEARS

Some bears are fierce, and some are fiercer.
Few bears (I rather hope) are near, sir.
From what I know of bears, they are
Better few and better far.

STILL MORE ABOUT BEARS

The fiercest bear of all is very
(A good thing, too) imaginary.
I say "a good thing" for, my dear,
If he were real, he might be here.

LAST WORD ABOUT BEARS

I meet few bears and few meet me.
But still it's my belief
That, meeting bears, the thing to be
Is—brief.

AT THE FARM

What would you say if I said I saw
A hen on the pond and a duck in the straw?

—I think I would say you had best go back
And see if that hen can say, "Quack! Quack!"

When that is done, you may try your luck
At asking that duck to say, "Cluck! Cluck!"

DAN DUNDER

Dan Dunder is a blunder.
What makes Dan so loud, I wonder?
If *I* knew how to be that loud
I think I'd look for a big black cloud
And get a job with it—as thunder!

HOW THE FRIGHTFUL CHILD GREW BETTER

Three tall Frowns
In caps and gowns
Were strolling south to Dover.
Three fat Grins
With double chins
Bumped them and knocked them over.

Two Hard Looks
Like iron hooks
Were glaring at the sky.
The sun broke through
A cloud and blew
A dazzle in their eye.

A Frightful Child
Was running wild
And screaming all day long.
Some Parents came
(You guess their name)
And told him it was wrong.

They told him and
They told him and
They told him and they told him.
Said Parent One
When it was done,
"It does no good to scold him."

Said Parent Two,
"Agreed. Will you
Please spank? He needs it badly."
Said Parent One,
"Dear Wife, Dear Son,
I'm at your service gladly."

He raised his hand,
He raised it and
He spanked him, as above.
Said One, said Two:
"Dear Son, may you
Accept this proof of love."

That Frightful Child
Grew sweet and mild,
And made them glad they'd got him.
Boys may seem bad
But a good dad
Can prove they're good—at bottom.

WHAT DO *YOU* THINK HIS DADDY DID?

Not in all of time, I think,
Has there been such a do, such a do, do, do,
As there was the day I spilled the ink,
The red ink, into my daddy's shoe.

The shoe was white, the ink was red.
But not as red as my daddy got
When he looked at me. And what he said
Was a little loud and a little hot.

No, not as loud and not as hot
As a gun going off with a boom, boom, boom.
But all the same he said a lot
Before he sent me up to my room.

. . . I am here in my room and I can't forget
What Daddy said. Not a word of it.
Forget? My goodness, no! Not yet.
So far I still can't sit!

WHAT DID YOU LEARN AT THE ZOO

What did I learn at the zoo?
Monkeys look like you.

Some are bald and some have curls,
But monkeys look like boys and girls.

Some are quiet and some make noise,
But all of them look like girls and boys.

What did *you* learn at the zoo?
Oh, much the same as you:

Gorillas are good, gorillas are bad,
But all of them look a lot like Dad.

Some do one thing, some another,
But all of them scream a lot like Mother.

What did *we* learn at the zoo?
Just what we wanted to:

That it's fun to tease if you make it rhyme
(Though you mustn't do it all the time),
That kangaroos hop and monkey's climb,
And that a bottle of lemon-and-lime
Is a very good way to spend a dime.

(And so is a bag of peanuts.)

TELL HIM TO GO HOME

Billy came to see us.
All he did was sing.
All he had to sing about
Was any old thing.

He sang about a mouse-trap
That sang about a mouse
That went to sea when it was three
And sailed around the house.

He sang about a cowboy
That sang about a cow
That sang all day about the hay
It smelled up in the mow.

He sang about a scare-crow
That sang about the scare
It got one night in the pale moon-light
When it woke to find *you* there.

He sang about a sheep-dog
That sang about a sheep
That sang a song that was so long
It sang itself to sleep.

Now Billy sleeps at our house
All he does is snore.
All he has to snore about
Is what he sang before.

He snores that it is night-time.
He snores that it is day.
I wish he'd snore a little more
And snore himself away.

THE BIRD-BRAIN SONG

Bird-Brain took a train
From Main-and-High to High-and-Main.
He paid his fare, got right on there,
Then got right off again,

Singing:
> A dollar for a stick of gum.
> A dollar for another.
> I paid a dime for the right time
> And gave it to my mother.

Bird-Brain, Bird-Brain, Bird-Brain, Bird,
Took a train from Second to Third.
He rode a block, then took a walk,
And now he's back—or so I've heard—

Singing:
> A dollar for a lollipop.
> Two dollars for the stick.
> I paid the rent with my last cent,
> And now I'm old and sick.

> My money's gone, I'm all alone.
> And now what shall I do?
> I'll sit and cry and hope that I
> May borrow some from you.

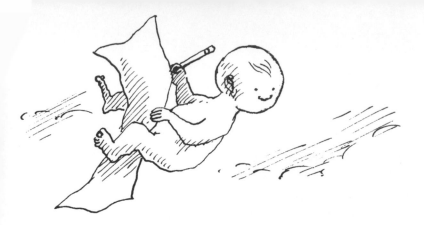

A SHORT CHECKLIST OF THINGS
TO THINK ABOUT BEFORE BEING BORN

The first thing you should think about
    When you go to the bother
Of being born is—picking out
    A father and a mother.

Next, when you've made up your mind
    You really would enjoy
Being a child—decide what kind.
    (That's mostly girl or boy.)

Study the immigration laws.
    Don't just go barging gaily in.
For it would give your parents pause
    If you were born an alien.

By now, of course, you should have planned
    Your family, if any—
Do you want sisters? brothers? and
    If you do, how many?

You may, if you are still in doubt,
    Skip one step or another.
But it just won't do to try without
    A father and a mother.

A DREAM ABOUT THE MAN IN THE MOON

Into my head
When I went to bed
Came a dream as fine as silk,
And it took me away
As if in play
To a land as white as milk.

The milk grew thin
As I looked in.
I took another look.
The milk was gone.
I was alone
By a little crooked brook.

The trees were blue.
The ducks said, "Hoo!"
The owls were taking a swim.
A frog said, "Why
Is your skin so dry?"
But I ran away from him.

I came to a dew
As sweet and new
As birthdays on a cake.
So I took a drink
And what do you think?—
The dew became a lake!

I drank it dry
And heard it cry,
"I'm going, going, gone!"
"Thanks for the drink,"
I said, "I think
I had best be going on."

I ran till noon
And found the moon
Asleep in the top of a tree.
"What! Sleep all day?"
I stopped to say,
"Why don't you shine?" Said he:

"I shine for the owl. I shine for the bat.
I shine for the fox. I shine for the cat.
I shine for the rabbits that dance in the dew.
What makes you think I should shine for you?

I shine for the sea, I shine for the land.
I shine for the frogs when they strike up the band
As they sit in the water all in a line.
Now you tell me—for whom do *you* shine?

I shine when the night-things come out of their den.
I shine for the fire-flies. I shine then
For the dog in the yard and the mice in the hall.
When do *you* shine—if you shine at all?"